Teaching Business English Online

The Conversation Method

by Gabriela Guzman

Teaching Business English Online

The Conversation Method

Copyright © 2019 by Gabriela Guzman

TABLE OF CONTENTS

INTRODUCTION

I have been teaching Business English online to foreign students for more than 5 years now. Prior to that, I taught business courses for more than 6 years as an adjunct at an online university in the United States for their business undergraduate department. However, when I started teaching English, I didn't have any experience teaching the language, let alone know the difference between an adverb and an adjective.

And frankly, I still don't. However, you don't really need to nowadays.

If you are a native English speaker, you can find an online teaching job anywhere. However, if you have some real-world business experience, then your job prospects are widened.

In this book, we will be discussing the general requirements that foreign online Business English schools look for when hiring teachers; from a college degree to teaching certifications that are recognized around the world. Not all schools have these requirements but for the most part, we will go over what they're looking for. In short, you will know what you need to have to get yourself an interview.

We will also be discussing the Conversation Method and how a course is structured using this technique. This is a really easy method that you will surely be using and is very popular with most online business and non-business English schools today.

I will review some topics that are essential to incorporate into your Business English class and go over a general lesson plan geared toward online business students that is applied to both group lessons and private lessons. These topics can help your students improve their business skills and/or land that job!

Also, essential tips and tricks will be discussed to help you practice and pass your demo. These tips can also keep students coming back for more lessons.

And lastly, I will also include some helpful teaching resources and online apps that will help you become a better teacher by helping your students in their English learning journey.

So, let's get started!

Requirements

First of all, let's go over some of the general requirements that most online English schools seek. Keep in mind not all schools have these requirements but it is best to be mindful of them as online English schools evolve.

One of the most important aspects of teaching business English is that you must know how to communicate professionally. Most lessons tend to be conversational but tailored toward professionals. In most cases, students are already well incorporated in the business world (i.e. CEO's and executives) and others want to improve their job prospects within the workplace.

Although most online schools stick to the conversation method, it is advisable that you have great writing skills. Some lessons for business English students may have some letter and resume writing lessons involved.

In addition to already having experience teaching English to adults, you would also need a Bachelor's degree (a 4-year University degree) or higher. The subject could be any, as long as you have the equivalent of a Bachelor's degree in your country. While some schools may prefer business majors, if you have real-world corporate experience, then the major will not matter. Most schools will ask for a copy of your transcripts or other type of proof but for the most part, a digital photo of the degree conferred is suffice.

Some schools will also ask for a TEFL, TESOL, or CELTA certification. Most will not but it is helpful if you do have one.

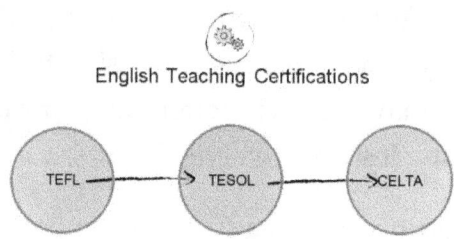

English Teaching Certifications

Let me give you the basics:

TEFL (Teaching English as a Foreign Language) is the most economical and less time consuming certification. You can get this from a variety of online English teaching schools in a matter of weeks. A 60-hour TEFL certificate can run anywhere from $150 to $2500, it just depends where you get it. Most TEFL courses can be taken online and once you've completed the assignments, the institution will grant you a teaching certificate.

There is also the 120-hour TEFL certificate if you wish to further your career. But if you're just looking for an online English teaching position to get by while you do something else, than the 60-hour TEFL is enough.

TEFL certifications will require classroom time, whether it's physically or online. However, I obtained my 60-hour TEFL certificate from El Cizne Language School (**www.elcizne.com**) and they did not require any classroom time.

It is also one of the most affordable ones on the market - at less than $100 dollars.

Check it out if you're a native English speaker and you need a TEFL certificate to get your foot in the door but you don't want to deal with the classroom time that most other institutions require.

Now, if you're looking to make teaching English a lifelong career, then the next two teaching certifications apply to you.

The TESOL (Teaching English to Speakers of Other Languages) certificate is a bit more intense as they do require actual in person classroom time. It's also longer than just few weeks and generally pricey as well. But if you want to make teaching English a fulltime career in the future, then I highly recommend this one. There are a variety of schools and the costs are a bit more prohibitive for most people. But if you have the time and money, why not give it a go?

The third option is the CELTA (Certificate in English Language Teaching to Adults) certification and is provided by the **Cambridge English Language Assessment,** specifically through authorized Cambridge English Teaching Qualification centers. CELTA was developed to be suitable both for those interested in Teaching English as a Foreign Language (TEFL) and Teaching English to the Speakers of Other Languages (TESOL).

CELTA is the UK and European standard certification. It can take months or a year or so to complete. Meaning it can get quite expensive. But again, if teaching English is your next career move, then go for it.

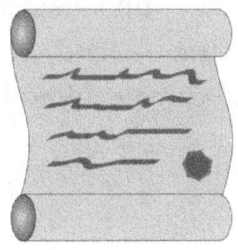

So there you have it. These are the top three internationally recognized certifications for teaching English around the world. It is up to you to decide which one works best for your needs.

CONVERSATION METHOD

The Conversation Method is the standard among online English business schools around the world. The focus of this method is on fluency and not necessarily grammatical correctness. Although grammar is taught in regular schools and universities, private language schools tend to focus on speaking and conversation skills.

The main focus of the conversation method is on functional communication activities and social interaction activities by asking questions tailored toward the student as well as role playing. Each learning style is different and the goal is to get students to contribute as much as they can. This helps them learn the language in an independent way.

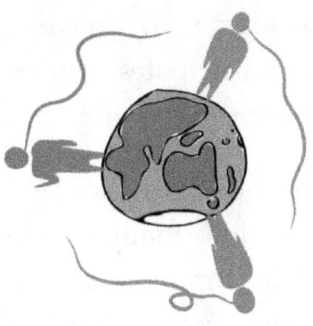

Although most online business schools prefer a neutral English accent, like a North American, most will be exposed to native English speakers who also have different accents depending on where they are from; such as British, Australian, South African and other accents from various native English speakers throughout their Business English learning experience.

For private one-on-one lessons, students chose the topic that they are most interested in discussing for their lesson. Otherwise, one is chosen for them.

The same goes for group lessons. Students usually work in groups of four to six students to make sure that everyone participates, whether in a formal or informal setting.

By the end of each lesson, students are assessed informally on their participation and understanding of what was discussed in class.

TOPICS FOR BUSINESS ENGLISH LESSONS

Business English learners tend to be advanced in their English speaking skills. Yet, they are looking for a way to be able to communicate effectively with their colleagues. Basically, how one would speak to friends is completely different from how one should speak with their coworkers and boss. Business English is about speaking appropriately and diplomatically around business professionals and in business situations.

This area covers a broad range of topics, such as how to write a resume. This is not to say that you are going to spend the entire class time writing your student's resume but rather guiding them on what should be included in one.

For example, as a teacher you can say that a resume includes one's objectives, education, experience and skill set. And the student would fill in the blanks and perhaps ask you for guidance on what they should or should not write.

Another topic that can be discussed would be interviews, either as an interviewee or as the interviewer.

Questions, such as:

"Where do you see yourself in 10 years from now?" or "Why should we hire you?" should be discussed.

These are great discussion questions either in a one to one setting or even incorporated in role playing in group classes. This can give your students a better idea as to how they will be answering these types of questions, should the need arise at some point in their professional career.

Other topics can include negotiating strategies and business etiquette for in person, phone or electronic communication. Another important area may be how to conduct meetings efficiently and how they can improve their presentation skills in the workforce.

The point is for students to gain more confidence while speaking English in the office and in the business world.

LESSON OUTLINE

In this chapter, we will look at a sample of what a lesson for business English students can look like. The lessons are usually already done for you, so you don't have to prepare them in advance, simply review them a few minutes before class begins.

For either private or group lessons, the outline is generally the same.

Introductions

We start off with the introductions. We like to say that this is the ice breaker moment. As the teacher, you introduce yourself with something like, your name, where you're from and how long you have been teaching English.

And then ask the student to do the same. Students may reciprocate by saying their name, where they are from and why they are learning English. Some may also include how long they have been learning the language.

While they are introducing themselves you can get a sense of their speaking level.

Then you will start off by reading the topic of that day's lesson.

In this case, the topic is Business Leadership.

You may want to ask students if they know what the word means and/or start them off by having them read the learning objectives.

For example:

"By the end of this lesson you will be able to: talk about different types of leaders. "

The introductions should take no more than 5 minutes and should be done at the beginning of the class.

Warm ups

Next, you move on to the Warm up section. You begin by asking questions or asking the students to describe what they see depending on the students level.

Warm Up
Answer the questions with your teacher and classmates.

- What kind of leader do you like at work? Why?
- Do you think the way someone leads is important? Explain
- Do different jobs need different kinds of leaders? Explain.

In this lesson, ask them questions like in the example above: What kind of leader do you like at work? Etc.

Vocabulary

You then introduce the student to new vocabulary. Usually around 5 but no more than 10 so that you don't overwhelm them.

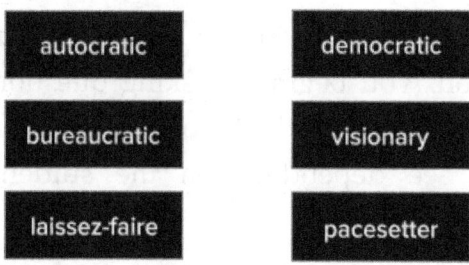

Activity

Some sort of activity usually precedes the vocabulary section to ensure the student understands the meaning of the words. Usually sentences that students need to fill in with the new vocabulary words or even a Mind Map illustration.

Reading

A little bit of reading doesn't hurt. So whether it's reading a paragraph, role playing or participating in a dialogue with another student, the point is to get them talking and using the English language. And if possible, the new vocabulary words.

Did you know: There are many leadership styles.

- The autocratic leader has total power and doesn't listen to anyone else.
- The *bureaucratic leader follows the rules and makes sure they are followed.
- A *laissez-faire leader leaves the employees alone to do things themselves.
- A democratic leader asks employees to come up with ideas and has them vote on decisions.
- A visionary leader tells where you are going but not how to get there.
- A pacesetter leads by example.

What kind of leader are you? Explain
Tell what kind of leader your boss is and compare with your classmates.

You can make minor corrections but don't overdo it. All you have to do is facilitate and make sure the students feel comfortable with the lesson.

Discussion

Near the end, you may have a discussion section, where you ask questions about the day's lesson.

Wrap up

At the end of the lesson, I usually like to ask students how they felt about the lesson. Was it easy, too difficult or just right?

At this time you also provide them with a bit of constructive feedback. And if they did really good, tell them how great they did!   Finally, say your good-byes and you're done with the lesson.

TIPS & TRICKS

Here, we will cover some tips and tricks that will help you pass your demo so that you can get an online teaching job.

Dress for success. Appear and dress professionally on camera. As an online Business English teacher, you want to project the image that you mean business, literally. Since Business English classes are tailored for those looking to sound more professional in their acquired language, you must practice what you preach in appearance.

Since you will be teaching online, try to wear a nice suit or top that is visible within your camera's viewpoint. Anywhere else that is out of your camera's range, you can wear whatever you want - even sweatpants.

Before you are hired, you will be asked to do a class demonstration (demo) that should illustrate how you will teach a class in the real world. Remember, this is your opportunity to shine!

A demo class is usually around 15-20 minutes long, about half or a third of what a normal class would be, with a 5-10 minute evaluation at the end. The final decision is usually made behind closed doors with an e-mail stating if you passed your demo or not.

The demo assessment is usually graded upon these four factors:

Lesson Preparation - How well you prepared yourself to teach the lesson. Most lessons are already done for you, you just have to put a little pizzazz and tailor it to your student's needs.

Teaching Attitude - Were you cheerful during your lesson? Was your student engaged or were they bored and fell asleep? Or worse... did your student hang up on you?!

Teaching Technique - How effective were you in making sure your student understood the lesson? Did you ask probing questions to make sure they understood?

Student Output - How involved was the student in your lesson? Was s/he asking questions? Were they responsive to the lesson?

Here are some tips that you can follow when you're teaching:

Be punctual - everyone hates people that are late. Try to be there about 5 minutes early before class begins and start to break the "ice" before class begins. Ask students about themselves or play some music in the background while you are waiting for class to begin.

Smile! - Always keep smiling. A smile goes a long way. Students can see and hear that smile in your voice. Be energetic but patient.

Be relatable! - Whenever possible, make the lesson about your students. Make it relatable so that they can engage in the lesson. Otherwise you will bore them to sleep if it's just a scripted lesson.

Use Teaching aids to engage and encourage your students.

Speak clearly and slow. Also make sure your instructions are simple.

Body Language - use your body language and be mindful of it. Be professional. Students can perceive your mood, even through a camera.

Above all...Have fun! Students can tell if you genuinely love your job or not. Because if you're not having fun while teaching a lesson, then this job is not for you. Keep that in mind.

Online Resources

There are many apps that can help you become a better teacher and can help your students learn faster.

Sites and apps like Dictionary.com and Webster.com, among others, provide a wealth of information, both for teachers and students. These sites can provide the definition of a word, its various meanings and similar words. It can also provide examples, such as how a certain word can be used in a sentence.

Words will have some type of phonetic spelling which can help students with the pronunciation of a word. As well as an audio clip of the word in question.

Google Translate is another great source for both students and teachers. While it is not perfect and sometimes the definition or meaning of a word may not be accurate, it is still a helpful tool as an add-on to other apps or online resources.

Online flashcards are also a great way to study.

Cram is a free flashcards app that is being used by millions of students and teachers as an aid for learning a new language and memorizing difficult concepts and subjects. It's very popular because of its easy-to-use interface and vast collection of flashcards.

Cram is useful in a multi-user classroom environment for teachers to create and share flashcard sets with their students. Teachers can add images and record their audio on each flashcard to teach proper pronunciation and improve the vocabulary of language learners.

Other apps like Duolingo, Busuu, Memrise and Babbel are hugely popular as well.

Duolingo is one of the world's most popular English language learning apps today. It is a FREE app and is highly recommended for English beginners. The gamified learning system of the app helps students learn English quickly while only spending twenty minutes a day. Duolingo structures their lessons in a way that teaches students to learn about seven new vocabulary words based on a topic and skill points that are awarded for completing each lesson.

Busuu is another FREE language learning app that covers the typical reading, writing, speaking and spelling concepts that students can expect in any language-learning lesson. Especially for beginners, it helps to know what the user will learn at that time, what they are expected to have learned by now, and what they will learn next. Lessons are structured so that students learn by building on what they already know, rather than being exposed to random and unconnected lessons in grammar, vocabulary, and so forth.

Memrise is my third choice and is a largely FREE language learning app. The focus of this app is to help users expand their vocabulary by learning English words in a effective way. The app also has courses to learn English grammar in an innovative way. You can even submit your own methods in order to keep the content fresh and share your ideas with other learners. You get to review each lesson multiple times after completion through a feature called spaced repetition testing. As an incentive to motivate learners, points are awarded for learning new words and completing each level. Memrise also offers an offline mode to continue learning without internet connection.

Babbel is not a free language learning app but it is relatively affordable. Babbel focuses on helping English language learners acquire basic conversational skills. Courses are divided into bite-sized lessons of 10 – 15 minutes each to give you just the right amount of learning time without overloading you with excess content. The app has four different approaches - Sound Recognition, Picture Recognition, Spelling and Fill in the blanks. Babbel also uses a custom goal system that allows users to set benchmarks as they learn a language and monitors their progress as well.

Lessons are divided into real-world topics so that students learn how to introduce themselves, order food, and make travel arrangements. Each word and phrase they learn can be used in the real world. This, Babbel says, is to ensure that students can start having real, meaningful conversations as soon as possible.

These and others are great on-the-go apps that can help your students learn English. You and your students will find out which ones suite your learning styles best.

CONCLUSION

I hope you have enjoyed reading this book as much as I have enjoyed writing it and putting it all together.

As I mentioned earlier, be mindful of each school's requirements. Most online business schools will require you to have experience teaching adults, at least a Bachelor's level degree and some type of English Teaching certification, like a TEFL. This one is the basic certification you will need to get your foot in the door at online language schools around the world.

Again, I highly recommend the 60-hour TEFL certificate from El Cizne Language School (**www.elcizne.com**), especially if you don't have the time to complete the course requirements that other institutions demand. Besides, you can't beat the price tag either!

Because most online schools will use the conversation method, the lessons will already be done for you. You just need to facilitate the course by making sure all students have had a chance to participate, tailor it to your students' needs and provide each student with a general assessment as to how they did in class that day.

Pay attention to the lesson outline and time constraints. Let students talk and ask you questions but don't linger too long on a single section, especially in group classes. Keep the class moving along, making minor corrections along the way.

My biggest tip is to always SMILE, make the lesson relatable and above all... Have Fun! Your students will be able to notice your enthusiasm!

There are a wealth of online resources and applications that can help you as a teacher to facilitate a class. Many tools are free so use them to your advantage.

I hope that this will help you on your journey to passing your demo and getting hired as an online Business English teacher, which is the ultimate goal of this book.

Good luck!